First Facts™

Our Physical World

Floating and Sinking

by Ellen Sturm Niz

Consultant:
Philip W. Hammer, PhD
Vice President, The Franklin Center
The Franklin Institute
Philadelphia, Pennsylvania

Capstone
press

Mankato, Minnesota

First Facts is published by Capstone Press,
151 Good Counsel Drive, P.O. Box 669, Mankato, Minnesota 56002.
www.capstonepress.com

Library of Congress Cataloging-in-Publication Data
Niz, Ellen Sturm.
    Floating and sinking / by Ellen Sturm Niz; consultant, Philip W. Hammer.
    p. cm.—(First facts. Our physical world)
    Includes bibliographical references and index.
    ISBN 13: 978-0-7368-5401-6 (hardcover)
    ISBN 10: 0-7368-5401-0 (hardcover)
    1. Floating bodies—Experiments—Juvenile literature. 2. Archimedes' principle
Experiments—Juvenile literature. I. Title. II. Series.
QC147.5.N59 2006
532'25'078—dc22   2005013322

Summary: Introduces young readers to the concepts of floating and sinking, and how they are
    used in the world. Includes instructions for an activity to demonstrate these concepts and
    their characteristics.

Editorial Credits
Aaron Sautter, editor; Linda Clavel, set designer; Bobbi J. Dey, book designer;
    Kelly Garvin, photo researcher/photo editor

Photo Credits
Brand X Pictures/Brian Hagiwara, cover (water)
Bruce Coleman Inc./Bob Burch, 14
Capstone Press/Karon Dubke, cover (toy boat and anchor), 6, 7, 10, 11, 21
Corbis/Ariel Skelley, 18; Grace/zefa, 5; Lester Lefkowitz, 17
Getty Images Inc./Time Life Pictures, 13
Peter Arnold, Inc./Carl R. Sams II, 9
Photo Researchers, Inc./Mark Garlick/Science Photo Library, 20
Seapics.com/David B. Fleetham, 15

Table of Contents

Floaters and Sinkers

If you toss a rock in a pond, it sinks. Throw a stick in the pond, and it will float. In **liquids** and **gases**, floaters rise up while sinkers fall down.

Solid objects are not the only things that sink or float. Liquids and gases can too. Balloons filled with helium gas float in the air. Water sinks when mixed with oil.

Density

An object's ability to float depends on its **density**. Objects float if they are less dense than the liquid or gas they are in. A wood boat floats because wood is less dense than water.

Objects sink if they are denser than the liquid or gas they are in. Metal coins sink in a water fountain because they are denser than the water.

Buoyancy

Buoyancy describes an object's ability to float. An object's buoyancy is determined by its density and shape. Thin, round lily pads are so buoyant that a frog can sit on them without sinking.

Buoyancy is also determined by the force of a liquid or gas pushing up on an object. Pond water pushes on the bottom of the lily pad to help it float.

> **! Fun Fact!**
> A child can lift an adult in a swimming pool because of the buoyant force of water.

Displacement

When you place floaters and sinkers in water, the water level rises. This happens because the objects move, or **displace**, some of the water.

Both sinkers and floaters displace water. This floating duck and the sinking rocks each displace some water. The duck floats higher when the water level rises.

Archimedes

More than 2,000 years ago, Greek scientist Archimedes studied floating objects. He noticed that the objects displaced some water, and that the water pushed up on the floaters.

He discovered that the force of water pushing up on floaters equals the weight of the water displaced. Today, this is called Archimedes' **Principle**. It works the same with all liquids and gases.

Fun Fact!
Archimedes first discovered displacement while taking a bath. He saw how he caused water to spill out of his bathtub.

Using Buoyancy

People can use buoyancy to float. Hot air balloons use hot air to float. Hot air is less dense than cold air. The hot air rises up, lifting the balloons into the sky.

Nature uses buoyancy too. Most fish have an air sac. The sac fills with air to help the fish float up in the water. It can empty out to let the fish swim deeper.

Making Sinkers Float

Changing a sinker's shape can help it float. A large block of steel sinks in water. But if the steel block is changed into a ship, it will float.

The shape of the ship covers a larger surface area. The water has a bigger area to push on. This makes the ship float.

Fun Fact!
Most ships have a line painted on them. The line helps sailors know when the ship is carrying too much weight to sail safely.

Floating and Sinking Safety

Floating on water can be fun. But it can also be dangerous. To stay safe in the water, people wear life jackets.

Life jackets are filled with foam. The foam is less dense than water. It helps you float and stay safe.

> **Fun Fact!**
> Astronauts train for space travel in huge swimming pools. The buoyancy of the water helps them float like they do in space.

Amazing but True!

Did you know that we are all floating right now? Earth's crust floats on a layer of hot, melted rock. At one time, earth's crust had just one big piece of land. Over millions of years, the land broke into several pieces. These pieces slowly floated apart to become today's seven continents.

Hands On: Will It Float?

Scientists learn about buoyancy by doing experiments. You can do your own experiments to see what floats and what sinks. Ask an adult to help you with this activity.

What You Need

household objects
large bowl
water
paper
pencil

What You Do

1. Gather some objects from around the house. Be sure they all fit in the large bowl. Have an adult help you choose the objects.
2. Make a list of what you think will float and sink.
3. Fill the large bowl with water. Leave about 2 inches (5 centimeters) of space at the top of the bowl.
4. Place each object in the bowl individually. Write down if the object floats or sinks.

Did you guess correctly? Why do you think the objects float or sink? Can you make the floaters sink or the sinkers float?

Glossary

buoyancy (BOY-uhn-see)—an object's ability to float; an object's buoyancy is determined by its density, shape, and the force of the liquid or gas pushing up on it.

density (DEN-si-tee)—the weight of an object compared to its size

displace (diss-PLAYSS)—to move something out of its normal position

gas (GASS)—a substance that will spread to fill any space that contains it

liquid (LIK-wid)—a wet substance that flows into, and takes the shape of, its container

principle (PRIN-suh-puhl)—a basic truth, law, or belief

Read More

Farndon, John. *Buoyancy.* Science Experiments. New York: Benchmark Books, 2002.

Nelson, Robin. *Float and Sink.* First Step Nonfiction. Minneapolis: Lerner, 2004.

Rosinsky, Natalie M. *Sinking and Floating.* Simply Science. Minneapolis: Compass Point Books, 2004.

Internet Sites

FactHound offers a safe, fun way to find Internet sites related to this book. All of the sites on FactHound have been researched by our staff.

Here's how:
1. Visit *www.facthound.com*
2. Type in this special code **0736854010** for age-appropriate sites. Or enter a search word related to this book for a more general search.
3. Click on the **Fetch It** button.

FactHound will fetch the best sites for you!

Index